Old Second Law

Jacob Kobina Ayiah Mensah

Contents

Author's Note

Fractal forms are very fascinating in the way they pose questions about the nature and human nature of life activity in the past, in the present and in the future. These forms are ubiquitous in nature and in human nature. I am searching for formulation to show this understanding by acting upon these questions, and by tracing such actions. These questions are visions becoming the highlights of this work written in English with Finnish, Swedish, Arabic, Spanish, Catalan, Basque, Malay, Tagalog, Chinese and Japanese to form a better comprehension of where these questions remain the space where we must be and where that space must look like. What are these questions? They are any questions that aid us to who we are. For examples: *How soon are we beginning to realise that we are differently same attachment of one cultural history? In what situation our face becomes our mind, and we see smell evaporating? Why our physical experience of the world is displayed alongside the pieces of our imagination?* This is a short collection of haiku with related materials written in more modernist style, dealing with such forms of objects and their situations in chaos and that illuminate parallel visions existing between the way the modern artist seeks to understand oneself and such actions. I have drawn on these questions about the processes of what we have built as a culture and the way we are seeing ourselves and which are necessary to a rational choice among those who can play the role in the pluralist defence of any art. For those who are defenders, the cultural significance of rational choice is itself the contribution to public knowledge. We establish our own tradition of understanding with no limit to the questions.

Part 1

In the monster's bones

on a sleepy ground
chasing sea crabs
old second law

throwing stones to the trees
and back to us
the distance of this morning sunlight

the statue of a soldier
waiting in the shower
to complete lacing his boots

black he-goat
and the old man battle each other
for the first light

going to the landlocked
a framed crow
from Turkey

the swindler in the market's voices
the golden ring in the pig's nose
made of mire

from a cock to a hen
the white darkness
that covers between

the breasts of a buxom
the body of flood waters
carrying my feet away

the vast land
is so small
in the ant's hole

the darkness in the corridor
waiting for a friend
to return from war

early morning raindrops
these arrows
from old China

the winds chew
the wine glass
and the wall looks on

in the moonlight
my shadow walks on
the green grass

hell is filled
with thousands of graves
and my anger

every stone here
has its life history
uprooted from elsewhere

at Apache Junction
a newspaper woman stops
drinks, eats and continues

lost ones
among news heroes
bailing violets and lilies

fly to Suddenland
on this motorbike
with 5000 cylinders

from Cobra Lane
to Oak Street
sand dispersing

to keep their histories
sea waves and shellfish
leaving the sea

light growing
from the seed husk
and memories darken

light growing
on the rocks
this green foliage

in Africa
a giant mark is drawn
between same flowers

childhood mire
moulded by
wild grass

in the monster's bones
I enter a world
full of greens and peace

old path
mounted on a stone
for few shadows to follow

I remember
my path
from the public square

spider-web
full of fog
and the rest of the city-lights

the sea wave listens
to its splashes
from within

in the sandstorm
a new journey
to the west

the cry of yellow butterfly
sinking
between my palms

a river
tracking its waste
from a new page

fall the space
needed to expand
the rain

petals in the street
within the reach
of the next door

a whore, a priest
and I
under an umbrella

Burning the margin

spring tide and the babbles that go through a bottle

the thread of misty fire burning the margin of dampness

paying the next premium the first figure I ever to create

erasing shorelines with a torch and now myself

colouring the shadows alongside the silence

misty harbour between shifting tides

erasing the shades of summer light from the hall

passed away this February attendees of crows

the colour only onions approaching in the sun

those mimosas evolving around the breath

the distance in the whirlwind becoming twice covered

in a pool in a full spoon this infinity

I tasted bitter persimmon and itself contained

wet winds sustained

nestling too late for the sun to set

庵のストレッチ

アスペンが震える闇を分ける

私のベッドで女性はまだ微笑んでいる

別のこの土壌の端の下で

池の近くに 音もなく散る花びら

月の穴は努力で満たされている

私の側のテーブルは霧がかかっているだけで十分です

His chopsticks and paintbrushes

at the meeting
someone lifts up
his chopsticks
and paintbrushes

questions moulded from the rice paddies

I bought many ears
together the crickets chirping
in someone's ears

out into the cold into the pines

sudden warm
are we coming
adrift

new proposal–
new friends show me
the capital of the stones

at dusk on a street
full of brothels
to choose from

                    in the mist between the heads

swatting the dust from left to right

sudden rain
sweeping away
our dry thoughts

back to the hermitage
the raindrop
finds its resting place

in a thatched hut
the grass is alive
to find me

rainwater dripping
through the crackles
to welcome me

a shy wild flower
is hiding its nakedness
in the morning sun

sitting in zazen
a widow returns
down the road

the ducklings follow the drake's footprints on footprints

everywhere this morning
butterflies, butterflies
dancing in circles

a step
from the hermitages
stretching between towns

my skin colour is soaked
in the sunny morning
empty street

in the entranceway
I greet water lilies
bending towards me

Hiroshima sunset
the faces I wrap
with a newspaper

farther north to Kamakura
farther north to the hill
this last weed

insects and small animals
outside listen
to poets conversing into the night

在女人的紧身衣之间，
古老的树林正在腐烂
给予新人

女性のタイツの間
では古い森が朽ちつつある
新しい人たちに与える

between a woman's tights
old woods are decaying
giving to new ones

the raindrops are drunk
after the rainfall

everything is sleeping
including this night

hiding away in an empty bottle
the rotten air from her egg

that blowfly
following
the odour smell
does not have
a high demand

a paper
too light to carry
but very heavy
in words from home

somewhere
in the rainclouds
I hear the crows cawing

the running water
without a map still
heading southward

even in the sun
that thin grass still
looking at the sun

in the inn there is a cricket
and a neighbour too
first mist

with the fire from the hearth
to the two in bed
the frames brighten

Part 2

Oberoende nyans

genom korridoren i en dagbok för att sluta någon annanstans

en fackla av fotsteg som lättar upp här

interiören genomsyras av ett glödande gult ljus

ekon av österländsk sol där ute

omringar den nedre kanten av ljus från alla hall

före smogen är jag ett annat klimat

dimman genom kioskens ridå

en kran slutar röra sig för nya

morgondagg på ytan av floden

Deep, deep down the blow

deep, deep down the blow
the smell of the violet
ahead of the black ants

afterglow
feet too heavy
to carry them away

beyond this moonlight
the distance sinks
into the mire

the parlour window
is dark
I follow my shadow on the floor

the grass is buzzing
in front of the chapel
turned into resident apartment

midnight raining
with a child's cry
and questions

long dawn
no mention of doors
or windows

late morning
the nurse looking at me
with her cheek-like tomatoes

for a second
lizards on the piled stones
mating and panting

smelling the rotten guava
how far is it
in this algebra

under the butterfly's shadow
the soft light waves spreading
and spreading

Floating behind

a bird
in my rib-cage
the whole evening in the street

cold bricks of the night between

claying out of sepulchre
I mould black in white
white in black

the artifact
on the potter's wheel
the softness against the gust

two rows of windows floating behind the heated moisture

cold and wet about zero and less than a thing

keeping a warm correspondence until the dust settle down

easy triumph perhaps in a neglected music on the florid stage

the finished statue waits for the unfinished ground

patters of the rain being part of the central vision

the grocery list of cabals and cliques and afterglow

on aisle 8 on the water bubble

                              scattered strawberries throughout the street after traffic jam

in the open library a paper crinkling from the corner

                         the sheet of Indian summer blitzing the hillside

dialing all possible variation from full graveyard

                         the shrapnel wounds deep into the warm evening

plunging off in a whole new direction from the metro

a kind of side trip outside the bar window

the tree with a halo between muggy nights

brighter streetlights emerging from the muddy clouds

traffic jam and segments of each agency

empty midnight street the screech and rumble to hold up

summer moonlit around the seeming landlocked

sharing the ribbiting of a toad with unfamiliar ears

late salesman folds the street to his corner

ocean foams stretching across the faded land

family tales among the fallen leaves

beside the bed the missing shadows

early snow occupying the space between us

the funeral day behind the darkness

Kiven läpi

makuulle lepäämään, kunnes varjo palaa kehoon

täysin uusi yhteisö valkoiset kivet

kiven läpi toinen kivi lepäämään

Another body

blue eyes and blond hair
arrived here
thousands of years ago

plunge into the lake
leafy birch twigs
return to another body

gleaming lights of downtown Helsinki
people and suburbs
side by side

18-hour nights of midwinter
gypsies, Jews and Turks
in one-family homes

smoked reindeer
side dish
on supper table

first snow in Helsinki darkens the hedgerow

in the voices something disappears again

on the ladder of rains from the wall

in the echo of the field another size of the lake

newspaper issues enclosing with green weeds

tying up the missing raindrops on the bare ground

through the stone through the hilliest region

on the offshore Aland Islands cold clouds wait

the dig in puritanical satisfaction

from fingering the strings to any recipe

utterly raw gin this early in Tuesday

the rosiest part of the noon forms its part

thinking of pink images of pulling motion

outside nothing you are right there

pairs of loosely
bound electrons
disturbing faith of yesterday

more force than you came out from yourself briefly

a very small NO process begins

many a saddle sustaining before the ruddy faces

from an equilibrium that seems on a close swathing of lace

figures stiffening in their necklets of dewdrops

stepping out of drifting off

this field full of receding hairlines

the void of music in the bottle drowning

autumn fan covers another smile

the ubiquity of loose border among the wet winds

outside this history
an unfluted dust
going unrecognized

pink dreams stretching on the hillside

near the abysmal waterdrops the new dwellings

the trellis around the foaming surf

on the floor a list of cold waterdrops from the history

screwing a word until it bears no further meaning

unwrapped issues as a common prayer now

one after the other rays of light on you

into her thirties i am too old to be her future

a dead thing to be called *beautiful callus* at dawn

coming here with phrases together

yellow dust moving across a field of dust

a long list of raindrops on the pavement

the windstorm settles for the bare minimum

the gipsy
the stallion and the rain
share a border shortly

around the neighbourhood of the Milky Way
a passage
through this seed husk

                            winter coldness slithering the streets of Hanoi

the first white lotus in front of the open garden

above autumn the illustrated home

the shape of red lotus flower in front of dusty garden

summer sunlight stains the beach

along the path potatoes struggle with the sunlight for space

the clouds of muddy road another place

the greens stretching darkeningly to the sea

gust and guests moaning at the party

light shimmers through the transparent floor

the rains nail at the louvre windows of this house

Part 3

Unang asul na petsa

isang mahabang gabi sa loob ng balat ng binhi

bawat isa ay umaamoy ng daanan sa bulok na prutas

unang asul na petsa at ang kalye ay masyadong malamig

From a newspaper

this morning unfolding from a newspaper

pressing a body of waters out of southeast planes for moonlight

at the bay in South East Asia, I keep autumn storms

Merenung dirinya sendiri

bandar banjir merenung dirinya sendiri

riak bayang-bayang putih di bawah

mimpi indah di antara dandelion

Whispering

rainwater gathering together in the sea

the grass whispering after a sharpened cutlass

surmounting barriers—
unobtrusive counterparts
to reduce the age gap

crabs spawning disagreement on the stones

one ear of the stone too hollow to swallow itself

forms return
from the noise
replacing the wet wind

behind the hidden truth the order in decaying

Una entrada no para todos

rostros distantes casi cerrándose detrás del espejo del vestidor

limitado por el calor
Gaudí edificios
y flamenco

en la escalera del lagarto y la antigua capilla

Coses tapes

1

una ombra al voltant de les ombres

fora de vista aquell carrer exposat

prop de la pedra de la llar
un pitó esperant
en la distància

2

Plaça de Catalunya
subway station
and its years along sides

blizzard on the next distract rearranges the pools

the slope leading up to my beginning

in the passable imitation of the fog

misty moors outside the fence

undulating passage somewhere under the clinking

the details of a branch of the tree this windstorm

the blowfly ahead of the rainclouds

on this journey to the place only a place becoming the next home

following the moist sand of the Braille

that whirlwind staying on its outmost wings

Hutsean

errepidean
Haizea jasotzen dut
eta ardo beltza

ate haizetsua
nire pisua herri hau da
saldu dut

ortzadarra
hondakinak ezkerrean daude

The rest of Monday

every stone is a god here
to watch
your tears

        whirlwinds around the womb in the vault

landlocked and the rest of Monday that flows out

       making hurricanes from the flattened towns

shadows floating among roofless houses

beyond the noises this town among the raindrops

too long from sideburn to astonished faces

expressive lips
caught in lovemaking
after a shortest day

the distance of the whirlwind completing with its disruption

only minimal winds in the rice field

المسافة بين

بالقرب من سطح مستو موسم جديد

أشعة الشمس تكشف عن نفسها كأشعة الشمس

عبر النافذة طائرة ورقية من الهالة

خلف موقف لا طائل منه هذا الندى المساء

المسافة بين نفس الأيدي بعيدة جدًا عن ذي
قبل

العاصفة الليلية المفاجئة إلى منطقة
أخرى

انعكاسات الضوء تملأ الفراغ

انعكاسات الضوء تملأ الفراغ

تلمع العيون بعيدًا عن الطماطم المتعفنة

على المنصة الخاطئة للمصباح الأمامي الجديد
الجديد

To love is to hate everything

I listen to your tears
children dance to them
and mothers follow

you have hidden
your naked body
in a tomato seed husk

your love is a clock
set in antique time
by the emperor's whore

palm weevils' emotions
are sonnets spreading
deeply in the swamp

the moonlit is solitude
a grey butterfly
holding itself firmly

lily flowers
are your captive
before the stars are born

I close my eyes and open
six months have gone
and a new corn on the market

at the gate
a popular water
will multiply soon

the footbridge—
the merest taste
among the apple trees

hilltop—
the vision of wild fields
from here

a white night
between brides
or mourners

in a box I welcome
my shadow
caught in another prison

lizards mating
each eyes
in a distant dream

field lily
once a water
and now the cold day

the boat on the lake
speaks to the fish
and the salt below

to love is to hate everything
this stillness of a dragonfly
in the wet morning